Windows 10 f

CW00841261

Release: 1.0.1.2a

Table of Contents

About Ordinary Human

Ordinary Human is a 20-year veteran of Microsoft who previously worked with various Microsoft teams to write documentation for Windows, Windows Server and other Microsoft products. If you have ever used any Microsoft product or operating system or had Microsoft training, you've probably seen Ordinary Human's work in action.

Ordinary Human pledges to update this manual from time to time to make corrections and changes as Windows 10 changes and to add content. How much time Ordinary Human can dedicate to the book depends on its readership and participation from readers like you.

Introduction

When it comes to technology and computers, ordinary humans often need a little help getting through the day. Sometimes ordinary humans wish training manuals had just the steps needed to get the job done and that's exactly what you'll find in this handy quick reference guide filled with step-by-step instructions and shortcuts for how to use Microsoft Windows 10.

Not only does this book provide a streamlined and concise learning experience, it is also an easy to use reference guide for any type of user that will help you get the job done quickly. Using this guide, you'll be able to:

- Teach yourself the essentials and latest features
- Learn how the new Windows works
- Work more efficiently with Windows 10
- Find just the tasks you need

Use the links provided in the Table of Contents at the end of this book to jump quickly to any task. Refer back to the Table of Contents to jump quickly to any other task. For example, on a kindle e-reader, slide in from the left to view the Table of Contents at any time.

Other resources I recommend for mastering Windows 10:

- Windows 10: The Personal Trainer by William Stanek
- Windows 10: Fast Start by Smart Brain Training Solutions

Both are excellent resources that will complement this book well.

Flying Start

Throughout this guide, where we use CLICK, RIGHT-CLICK and DOUBLE-CLICK, you can use the touch equivalents of TAP, PRESS AND HOLD and DOUBLE TAP. HOVER means to position the mouse over the designated item without CLICKing.

When working in Tablet mode, CLICK START should be replaced with CLICK ☰ on the START screen.

🪟 This is the Windows Logo Key on your keyboard. Press this key in combination with other keys to access keyboard shortcuts. Press this key by itself to display or hide Start.

Starting Windows

1. CLICK or SWIPE UP on the starting picture.
2. If necessary, select a user.
3. If necessary, CLICK Sign-In Options and select an alternate sign-in method:

🖼 **Picture**. Draw the password gestures in the correct sequence.

🔑 **Password**. Type the password and then PRESS Enter or CLICK →..

 **PIN**. Type the PIN.

For a password or PIN, CLICK ![eye icon] to reveal what you've typed. If your computer is used for business or has special hardware, you may have additional options for scanning your fingerprint, face or iris.

Switching Users

If your computer has multiple user accounts, you can switch to another user without having to log out. Switching users saves your work and allows another user to log in. Then when the user is finished using the computer, the user can sign out and you can sign in again and resume your work.

To switch users, CLICK START, ![user icon] and choose the user to switch with.

Working with Tablet Mode

When you're using Windows 10 on a tablet, tablet mode is enabled by default. With tablet mode, your device has a Start screen instead of a Start menu, app icons are hidden on the taskbar and apps open in full-screen mode. Further, the Start screen is displayed when you login instead of the desktop.

To display app icons on the taskbar when using tablet mode,

CLICK START, ![settings gear icon] , System, Tablet Mode. Next, CLICK Hide App Icons... setting it to the OFF position.

To go to the desktop instead of Start when you login, CLICK

START, , System, Tablet Mode. Next, CLICK When I Sign In... setting it to the OFF position.

If you don't want to use tablet mode, CLICK START, 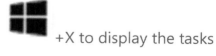, System, Tablet Mode. Next, CLICK Make Windows More Friendly... setting it to the OFF position.

Performing Common Tasks Quickly

Programs and Features
Power Options
Event Viewer
System
Device Manager
Network Connections
Disk Management
Computer Management
Command Prompt
Command Prompt (Admin)

Task Manager
Control Panel
File Explorer
Search
Run

Shut down or sign out   >
Desktop

1. RIGHT-CLICK Start or PRESS  +X to display the tasks menu.
2. CLICK to open an item.

> **Tip:** Like PowerShell instead of Command Prompt? Replace Command Prompt items with PowerShell options in the tasks menu: RIGHT-CLICK an open area on the taskbar, CLICK Properties. Next CLICK Navigation and then CLICK Replace Command Prompt with Windows PowerShell.

Locking Your Screen

Protect your work when you step away from your computer by locking your screen. Keep in mind that locking your screen doesn't end your Windows session. Instead, your device pauses the session and you resume the session by unlocking the screen.

To lock your screen, CLICK START, and choose Lock. Or PRESS  + L.

To unlock your screen, CLICK or SWIPE UP anywhere on the screen, enter your password, then PRESS Enter or CLICK .

Exiting Windows

When you are done using your computer, you can end your Windows session by signing out or turning off the device. You have two options for turning off the device:

- **Sleep**   The device enters a low-power state.
- **Shutdown**   The device powers off completely.

To sign out, CLICK START, , then choose SIGN OUT.

To sleep or shutdown, CLICK START, , then choose either SLEEP or SHUT DOWN.

The Big Changes

Windows 10 provides a unified experience whether you are using a smartphone, an Xbox, a laptop PC, a desktop PC or a tablet PC. To sync your settings between devices, you must use a connected account and then log-in using the same account. The standard type of connected account is a Microsoft account.

It's easy to distinguish a Microsoft account from a local computer account. Microsoft accounts have a username@domainname format, such as OrdinaryHuman.Books@gmail.com. Local computer accounts just have a user name, such as OrdinaryHuman.

In the very cool department, Windows 10 supports multiple monitors and multiple desktops. Multiple monitors allow you to connect two or more displays to your device and stretch the desktop across those monitors so you can use all of the screen real estate. Multiple desktops allow you to create additional workspaces and switch between those workspaces at any time by CLICKing the Task View button. Each workspace is a virtual desktop. Although you can have as many virtual desktops as you want, each desktop uses system resources and you'll usually want to limit the number of virtual desktops.

Other big changes:

- File Explorer has replaced Windows Explorer.
- Edge browser has replaced Internet Explorer
- Settings has replaced most Control Panel functionality.
- Search has been rebuilt and now incorporates Cortana, a virtual assistant technology.

If you have a tablet or smartphone, your device will use tablet mode by default, which is different from the standard mode used by desktops and laptops. See **Working with Tablet Mode**.

Apps and Start

Start is split into two vertical columns with apps and options on the left and app tiles on the right. The left-side options include:

Displays account options: Change Account Settings, Lock, Sign Out. Also lets you switch to another user by CLICKing their name.

Opens File Explorer. Use File Explorer to browse your device's drives and folders.

Opens Settings. Use Settings to configure Windows on your device.

Displays power options: Sleep, Shut Down and Restart.

Displays the All Apps view on Start, which replaces items in the left column. The All Apps view is an A – Z list of installed apps.

> **NOTE**: Use Search instead of All Apps to find an app
>
> quickly. See **Searching for Apps**.

Personalizing Start

You can personalize Start by changing its default options.

1. CLICK START, SETTINGS, PERSONALIZATION, START.
2. CLICK to turn on/off the Most Used or Recently Used apps lists.
3. CLICK to turn on/off Jump Lists (which show recently used files, common tasks, etc) for pinned apps whether on the Start menu or on the taskbar.
4. CLICK Choose Which Folders Appear On Start to add or remove pinned folders for File Explorer, Settings, etc.

Resizing Start

1. HOVER over the edge of the Start menu. The mouse pointer changes to the resizing pointer, showing arrows facing left and right.
2. DRAG the edge to increase or decrease the size of the Start menu.

Managing Tile Groups

Start has two tile groups, each with a default name. You can create additional tile groups.

To create a new group:

1. DRAG a tile below or to the right of an existing tile group until a new group title bar appears.
2. HOVER over the new tile group's title and then CLICK the default title.
3. Type a name then PRESS Enter.

To change the name of a tile group:

1. CLICK the name.
2. Delete or modify the existing text as appropriate.
3. Type the desired name and then PRESS Enter.

To rearrange a tile group, DRAG its title bar to a new location.

Resizing Tiles

Windows 10 has standard tiles and live tiles. The difference between the two is that live tiles display live contents that can be updated when you have an Internet connection and standard tiles display static content that isn't updated. Most tiles can be resized to small (70x70), medium (150x150), wide (310x150) or large (310x310).

- RIGHT-CLICK the tile, choose Resize, then select a size.
- Or PRESS AND HOLD the tile, TAP the options button, then select a size.

Moving Tiles

- DRAG a tile to a new position to move it.

- Or PRESS AND HOLD the tile then DRAG it to a new position.

Pinning Apps on Start

You create new tiles on Start by pinning apps.

1. On the Start menu, CLICK the All Apps option, then locate the app in the list.

2. RIGHT-CLICK the app in the list, then select Pin To Start.

Or use File Explorer to locate the item that you want to pin, RIGHT CLICK it, then CLICK Pin To Start.

To remove a pinned item:

- RIGHT-CLICK it, then select Unpin From Start.
- Or PRESS AND HOLD then CLICK the Pin button.

Searching for Apps, Settings and More

The Search box allows you to quickly search for Apps, Settings, options in Control Panel, personal files, and web sites. Initiate a search simply by typing when the Start menu is open or by CLICKING in the Search box and then typing.

The Search box is displayed on the taskbar by default, except in tablet mode.

Here, CLICK to begin a search and then type.

Apps and the Taskbar

Windows 10 displays various icons on the taskbar depending on the open apps, operating mode and installed hardware. In the example, the device is in tablet mode.

Opens the Start menu or displays the Start screen.

In tablet mode, allows you to go back to the previous app or window.

In tablet mode, starts a search.

Displays or hides the task view, which allows you to quickly select an open app or window.

Displays information about network connections and allows you to access network settings.

Displays audio levels for speakers or headphones and allows you to adjust them.

Displays new notifications from Action Center. This includes alerts about security and maintenance.

When you are working in standard mode with a device running on battery power, you'll have more options, including those for working with battery-related settings and Wi-Fi.

Opens the system tray and displays icons for apps running in the background. CLICK an icon to open the related app or display an options menu. Alternatively, RIGHT-CLICK an icon to display its options menu.

> **NOTE**: If your device has Bluetooth, you'll find a related system icon. CLICK Show Hidden Icons, Bluetooth Devices, Open Settings to manage Bluetooth options. To enable Bluetooth, select the Allow Bluetooth... option. To disable Bluetooth, clear this option.

Shows remaining battery power and provides access to related settings, such as screen brightness, power & sleep settings. Click Battery Saver to enter or exit battery-saver mode.

Displays information about wireless networks and allows you to access network settings. CLICK Airplane Mode to enter or exit a protected mode that disables all network connections.

Displays the Onscreen Keyboard. With touch devices, this is a handy option to have on the taskbar.

Configuring the Taskbar

You can customize the taskbar in several ways:

- RIGHT-CLICK and then select Show Task View Button or Show Touch Keyboard Button to control whether the buttons appear on the taskbar.
- RIGHT-CLICK, select Toolbars and then select Address, Links or Desktop to control whether the related toolbars appear on the taskbar. Alternatively, select New Toolbar to choose a folder to add as a toolbar.
- RIGHT-CLICK, select Properties and then use the Taskbar Buttons options to control taskbar buttons are always combined, combined only when the taskbar is full, or never combined.
- RIGHT-CLICK, select Properties and then CLICK Customize in the Notification Area. Next, CLICK Select Which Icons Appear On The Taskbar. Use the options provided to specify which icons are displayed in the notification area.

App icons aren't displayed on the taskbar when using tablet

mode. To display app icons, CLICK START, , System, Tablet Mode. Next, CLICK Hide App Icons... setting it to the OFF position.

Moving the Taskbar

By default, the taskbar is locked to prevent you from accidentally moving or hiding it. To unlock the taskbar, RIGHT-CLICK an open area on the taskbar and then select Lock The Taskbar to clear the checkmark.

With the taskbar unlocked, you can move it by CLICKING on it and DRAGGING.

- DRAG the taskbar to the left or right to dock it on the left or right.
- DRAG up to dock the taskbar to the top of the desktop.

After you position the taskbar lock it by RIGHT-CLICKING an open area on the taskbar and then selecting Lock The Taskbar to add the checkmark.

Pinning Apps to the Taskbar

1. On the Start menu, CLICK the All Apps option.

2. RIGHT-CLICK the app in the list, then select Pin To Taskbar.

Or use File Explorer to locate the app that you want to pin, RIGHT CLICK it, and then CLICK Pin To Taskbar.

To remove a pinned app, RIGHT-CLICK it and then select Unpin This Program From Taskbar.

To rearrange pinned apps, DRAG an app to a new taskbar location.

Using Taskbar Jump Lists

Jump lists show frequently or recently used files, pinned files, commonly performed tasks and other options. SWIPE UP or RIGHT-CLICK an item on the taskbar to display its jump list.

TIP: Sometimes, you'll need to run pinned apps with administrator privileges. To do this, RIGHT-CLICK the app, then in the jump list RIGHT-CLICK the app name. If the app can run with administrator privileges, a second jump list will have a Run As Administrator option which you can select. For example, you can use this with Command Prompt or the Windows PowerShell prompt when they are pinned to the taskbar.

Action Center and Notifications

Open Action Center by CLICKING  on the taskbar or SWIPING IN from the right screen edge.

Action Center provides notifications about security, maintenance and system issues. Action Center notifications display icons that tell you their purpose. Alerts have warning icons.

Using Action Center

Respond to each notification as appropriate:

- CLICK or HOVER and then CLICK to expand the notification and get more details.

- CLICK or HOVER and then CLICK to close the notification.
- CLICK Clear All to remove all messages.

Using Quick Action Buttons

Quick Action buttons in Action Center allow you to perform certain actions quickly. The buttons you see depend on the type of device you are using and its hardware and can include:

- **Battery Saver**   Changes system settings to reduce power consumption. Manage battery saver settings: CLICK Start, Settings, System, Battery Saver, Battery Saver Settings. Then configure the desired settings.
- **Connect**   Connects to wireless devices using Bluetooth and similar technologies.
- **Location**   Displays information about the current location.
- **Quiet Hours**   Turns off notifications and messages until you remove the Quiet Hours option.
- **Tablet Mode**   Enables or disables Tablet mode. See **Working With Tablet Mode**.
- **VPN**   Provides quick access to a workplace connection over VPN.

Use Collapse to collapse the quick action buttons to a single row and show more notifications.

Use Expand to expand the quick action area to two rows and show more buttons.

Configure the button default options: CLICK Start, , System, Notifications & Action, Quick Actions. Then CLICK each button in turn and select its default action.

Starting and Using Apps

CLICK Start, then CLICK the app tile to start an app. Or use these techniques:

- CLICK Start, CLICK , CLICK the app.
- CLICK the app shortcut on the taskbar.

Opening App Files

1. PRESS CTRL + O or CLICK File, then CLICK Open.
2. CLICK Computer, CLICK Browse.
3. Find your file. CLICK Open.

Copying and Pasting Text

1. DRAG over the words in the text to highlight them.
2. RIGHT-CLICK then select Copy.
3. RIGHT-CLICK where you want to paste the text, then select Paste.

You can also:

1. TAP a word in the text to copy.
2. DRAG the circles at each end of the highlighted text.
3. TAP Copy.
4. TAP where you want to paste, then select Paste.

Saving New App Files

1. PRESS CTRL + S or CLICK File, then CLICK Save As.
2. CLICK Computer, CLICK Browse.
3. Select a save location, type a file name, CLICK Save.

Saving App Files in the Current Location

- PRESS CTRL + S or CLICK File, then CLICK Save.

Adding Files or Folders to the Desktop

1. CLICK on the taskbar.
2. RIGHT-CLICK the file or folder after locating it.
3. CLICK Send To, Desktop (Create Shortcut).

Adding System Icons to the Desktop

1. RIGHT-CLICK an open area of the desktop, CLICK Personalize.
2. Select the icons to add, such as Computer and Control Panel.

Switching Between Apps or Windows

- PRESS AND HOLD ALT, then PRESS TAB until app is selected.
- SLIDE IN from left, then TAP the app to use.

- CLICK to open previous app.

You can also:

1. PRESS AND HOLD to show recently used apps.
2. SWIPE between them, TAP the app to use.

Using Task View to Switch Apps

1. PRESS ALT + TAB.
2. CLICK the app to use.

Close Current App

- CLICK in the upper-right corner.

Close Other Apps

1. PRESS AND HOLD ALT, then PRESS TAB until app is selected.

2. While HOLDING ALT, HOVER over app and CLICK .

You can also:

1. PRESS AND HOLD to show recently used apps.
2. SWIPE down on any app to close it.

Managing Apps

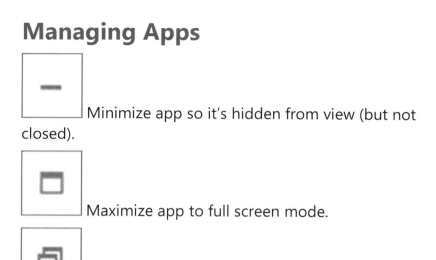

Minimize app so it's hidden from view (but not closed).

Maximize app to full screen mode.

Exit full screen mode.

Close the app.

You also can close apps using the taskbar. RIGHT-CLICK then select Close Window.

Installing Apps

1. CLICK , locate an app to install.
2. CLICK the BUY option.

Completing App Downloads

Apps you've purchased are queued to be downloaded and installed. If the download doesn't complete automatically, you'll need to restart it:

1. CLICK . Next, CLICK ![icon], then CLICK Downloads.
2. CLICK the app, then CLICK Retry.

Resizing App Windows

1. CLICK ![icon] to exit full screen mode, if necessary.
2. HOVER over the left/right or top/bottom edge of the window. The mouse pointer changes to the resizing pointer, showing arrows facing left and right.
3. DRAG the edge to increase or decrease the size of the window.

Arranging Apps Side by Side

Snap is a feature of Windows 10 that allows you to arrange apps side by side or to toggle the view of an app between its standard view and snapped view.

- ![Windows key] **+ Left Arrow**   Snaps apps to the left side of screen (or toggles to its standard view).

- ![Windows key] **+ Right Arrow**   Snaps app to the right side of the screen (or toggles to its standard view).

-
- ![Windows key] **+ Up Arrow**   Displays the app in Full Screen mode (or positions a snapped app in the upper corner so that another app can be displayed in the lower corner).

-  **+ Down Arrow** Exits Full Screen mode and returns the app to its original window state (or positions a snapped app in the lower corner so that another app can be displayed in the upper corner).

> **Tip:** Configure snap behavior: CLICK Start, Settings, System, Multitasking. Then use the options provided to manage the way snap works.

Checking for App Updates

Apps you've purchased can be updated periodically by the developer. Normally, app updates are installed automatically, if you have a Wi-Fi connection. To check for updates manually:

1. CLICK ![store icon]. Next, CLICK ![account icon], then CLICK Downloads.
2. CLICK Check For Updates.

Uninstalling Apps

1. RIGHT-CLICK on the desktop. CLICK Display Settings. CLICK Apps & Features.
2. CLICK the app to uninstall, then CLICK Uninstall.

Using Cortana for Search

Cortana is your virtual assistant to help you with searches and the first time you use search you can configure this feature. CLICK Next and follow the prompts. Otherwise, CLICK Not Interested to close Cortana (and not use the feature in the future).

If you don't configure Cortana and want to use this feature later:

1. CLICK in the Search box. Then CLICK .
2. CLICK Cortana Can Give You Suggestions... to toggle the feature to On.
3. CLICK Next, then follow the prompts.

To search using Cortana, simply start typing when the Start menu is open or CLICK in the Search box and then start typing.

Search results show related installed apps first, settings next and then apps in the Microsoft Store.

> **Tip:** Online and web results are included by default in search results. Want results only from Settings, Control Panel, personal files, and apps? CLICK in the Search box
>
> and then CLICK . Next CLICK Search Online And Include Web Results to toggle the feature to Off.

Using the Onscreen Keyboard

The onscreen keyboard is useful for devices without a dedicated keyboard. The keyboard opens automatically anytime you TAP in an area where text input is selected. You also can open the keyboard by CLICKING the touch keyboard button on the taskbar.

- TAP AND HOLD shift to enable/disable caps lock.
- TAP AND HOLD vowels to see common accents.
- TAP AND HOLD symbols to see related symbols.

Adding a Keyboard Button to the Taskbar

1. RIGHT-CLICK an open area of the taskbar.
2. CLICK Show Touch Keyboard Button.

Moving the Onscreen Keyboard

1. If the keyboard is docked at the bottom of the screen,

CLICK .

2. DRAG the keyboard to the desired location.

Creating and Managing Desktops

Window 10 supports multiple virtual desktops. Each virtual desktop provides a separate working space where you can have open apps and windows.

Creating a New Desktop

1. CLICK or PRESS + TAB.
2. CLICK New Desktop.
3. CLICK the desktop to use.

Opening an App on a Different Desktop

1. CLICK or PRESS + TAB.
2. CLICK the desktop to use.

3. CLICK Start, .
4. CLICK the app to open.

Going to a Different Desktop

1. CLICK or PRESS + TAB.
2. CLICK the desktop to use.

Closing a Desktop

1. CLICK  or PRESS ⊞ + TAB.

2. HOVER over the desktop thumbnail, then CLICK ☒.

3. Any open apps or windows are moved to the previous desktop.

Working with Files and Folders

File Explorer has replaced Windows Explorer for working with files and folders. To open File Explorer:

- CLICK on the taskbar.
- Or RIGHT-CLICK Start, then CLICK File Explorer.
- Or TYPE File Explorer in the Search box, then PRESS Enter.

To open additional File Explorer windows:

1. RIGHT-CLICK on the taskbar.
2. CLICK File Explorer on the jump list.

Creating a Folder

1. RIGHT-CLICK an open area in File Explorer.
2. CLICK New, Folder.

Selecting Files and Folders

Select multiple items one at a time:

1. PRESS AND HOLD CTRL.
2. CLICK each item to select.

Select multiple items in a group:

1. PRESS AND HOLD SHIFT.
2. CLICK first item, then CLICK the last.

Zipping Files and Folders

1. Select items to zip. See **Selecting Files and Folders**.

2. RIGHT-CLICK, then CLICK Send To, Compressed (Zipped) Folder.
3. Type a name for the Zipped folder.
4. Press ENTER or CLICK elsewhere.

Unzipping (Extracting) Files and Folders

1. RIGHT-CLICK the zipped folder.
2. CLICK Extract All, Browse.
3. Select an extraction location, then CLICK Select Folder.
4. CLICK Extract.

Copying Files and Folders

1. Select items to copy. See **Selecting Files and Folders**.
2. PRESS AND HOLD CTRL, then drag to new location.

Moving Files and Folders

1. Select items to move. See **Selecting Files and Folders**.
2. Drag to new location on same drive.

Tip: PRESS AND HOLD SHIFT before releasing to move to a different drive (rather than copy).

Copying and Pasting Files and Folders

1. Select items to copy. See **Selecting Files and Folders**.
2. RIGHT-CLICK, then select Copy or PRESS Ctrl+C.
3. In the copy location, RIGHT-CLICK, then select Paste or PRESS Ctrl+V.

Cutting and Pasting Files and Folders

1. Select items to move. See **Selecting Files and Folders**.
2. RIGHT-CLICK, then select Cut or PRESS Ctrl+X.
3. In the move location, RIGHT-CLICK, then select Paste or PRESS Ctrl+V.

Renaming a File or Folder

1. RIGHT-CLICK the file or folder, then select Rename.
2. Type the new name.
3. Press Enter or TAP.

Creating and Using Desktop Shortcuts

Shortcuts help you quickly open apps, files and folders. To create a shortcut:

1. RIGHT-CLICK the app, file or folder.
2. CLICK Send To, Desktop (Create Shortcut)

DOUBLE-CLICK the shortcut to open the related item.

Deleting a File or Folder

- RIGHT-CLICK the file or folder, then select Delete.
- Or CLICK the file or folder, then PRESS DELETE.

Tip: Windows 10 moves deleted items to Recycle Bin by default. To permanently delete, empty Recycle Bin. To delete a file immediately and bypass Recycle Bin, PRESS SHIFT + DELETE.

Searching for Files and Folders

File Explorer provides built-in search functionality. To perform a basic search:

1. Select a starting location.
2. CLICK in the Search box in File Explorer.
3. TYPE your search text, then PRESS ENTER.

Searching by Date Modified

1. Open File Explorer, then select a starting location.
2. CLICK in the Search box in File Explorer.
3. On the toolbar, CLICK Search, Date Modified.
4. Select a preset date: Today, Yesterday, This Week, Last Week, etc.
5. TYPE your search text, then PRESS ENTER.

Searching by Kind of File

1. Open File Explorer, then select a starting location.
2. CLICK in the Search box in File Explorer.
3. On the toolbar, CLICK Search, Kind.
4. Select the type of file, such as Picture, Music or Video
5. TYPE your search text, then PRESS ENTER.

Searching by File Size

1. Open File Explorer, then select a starting location.
2. CLICK in the Search box in File Explorer.
3. On the toolbar, CLICK Search, Size.
4. Select the size of the file, such as Small (10 – 100 KB) or Large (1 – 16 MB).
5. TYPE your search text, then PRESS ENTER.

Working with Recycle Bin

Windows 10 moves deleted items to Recycle Bin by default, giving you the option to restore deleted items to recover them if necessary. To open Recycle Bin:

- TYPE Recycle Bin in the Search box, then PRESS ENTER.
- Or DOUBLE-CLICK Recycle Bin on the desktop to open it.

Restoring a Deleted Item

1. TYPE Recycle Bin in the Search box, then PRESS ENTER.
2. RIGHT-CLICK item to restore, then select Restore.

Restoring Multiple Deleted Items

1. TYPE Recycle Bin in the Search box, then PRESS ENTER.
2. Select items to restore. See **Selecting Files and Folders**.
3. RIGHT-CLICK, then select Restore.

Restoring All Deleted Items

1. TYPE Recycle Bin in the Search box, then PRESS ENTER.
2. CLICK Mange on the toolbar, then select Restore All Items.

Emptying the Recycle Bin

1. TYPE Recycle Bin in the Search box, then PRESS ENTER.
2. CLICK Mange on the toolbar, then select Empty Recycle Bin.

Protecting Your Files From Accidental Deletion

It's easy to accidentally delete files and folders. If you do this frequently, you may want Windows to prompt you before deleting files:

1. TYPE Recycle Bin in the Search box then PRESS ENTER.
2. CLICK Mange on the toolbar, then select Recycle Bin
   Properties.
3. Select Display Delete Confirmation Dialog.

Settings and Troubleshooting

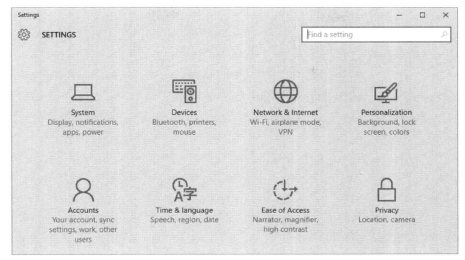

Although Control Panel remains available, Settings is the primary utility for customizing settings and options. To open Settings:

- CLICK Start, .
- Or TYPE Settings in the Search box, then PRESS Enter.

Getting Information About Your Device

1. RIGHT-CLICK on the desktop, CLICK Display Settings.
2. CLICK About to see information about your device's configuration.

Checking for Windows Updates

1. CLICK Start, ⚙, then CLICK Updates & Security.
2. CLICK Check For Updates.

Quitting Nonresponsive Apps

1. RIGHT-CLICK Start, then CLICK Task Manager.
2. RIGHT-CLICK the nonresponsive app in Task Manager.
3. CLICK End Task.

Changing Battery Saver Settings

1. RIGHT-CLICK on the desktop. CLICK Display Settings. CLICK
   Battery Saver.
2. CLICK Battery Saver Settings.
3. Use the settings provided to control battery saving options.

Renaming Your Device

1. RIGHT-CLICK on the desktop. CLICK Display Settings. CLICK
   About.
2. CLICK Rename PC.
3. TYPE the new name, then CLICK Next.
4. CLICK Restart Now.

Asking for Help

1. TYPE Invite Someone to Help in the Search box, then PRESS
   Enter.
2. CLICK Invite Someone You Trust To Help You, then follow
   the prompts.

Customizing Your Desktop and Lock Screen

The desktop and lock screen can be customized to meet your needs.

Customizing Your Desktop Background

1. RIGHT-CLICK on the desktop. CLICK Personalize.
2. CLICK the Background list, then select Picture or Solid Color.
3. CLICK the picture or color to use.
4. With pictures, CLICK Choose A Fit, then CLICK the desired fit.

Using Picture Slideshows for Desktop Backgrounds

1. RIGHT-CLICK on the desktop, CLICK Personalize.
2. CLICK the Background list, then CLICK Slideshow.
3. CLICK Browse, then select a source location.
4. CLICK Change Picture Every, then select a change option, such as 30 minutes.
5. CLICK Choose A Fit, then CLICK the desired fit.

Note: Your Pictures library is the default source.

Customizing Your Lock Screen

1. RIGHT-CLICK on the desktop. CLICK Personalize. CLICK Lock Screen.
2. CLICK the Background list, then select Picture.
3. CLICK the picture to use.

Using Picture Slideshows on the Lock Screen

1. RIGHT-CLICK on the desktop. CLICK Personalize. CLICK Lock Screen.
2. CLICK the Background list, then CLICK Windows Spotlight or Slideshow.
3. If you selected Slideshow, CLICK Add A Folder and then select a source location.

Your Pictures library is the default source. To remove a source folder, CLICK it, then CLICK Remove.

Configuring Screen Timeout

1. RIGHT-CLICK on the desktop. CLICK Display Settings. CLICK Power & Sleep.
2. Under SCREEN, CLICK the On Battery and Plugged In lists and then select a turn off after value.

Configuring Sleep Settings

1. RIGHT-CLICK on the desktop. CLICK Display Settings. CLICK Power & Sleep.
2. Under SLEEP, CLICK the On Battery and Plugged In lists and then select a sleep after value.

User Accounts and Security Settings

Your device can have several types of user accounts:

- **Local** Local user accounts are created only on your device.
- **Domain** Domain user accounts are created when your device is connected to a domain.
- **Connected** Connected user accounts are created when you add a Microsoft account to your device.

Note: Connected user accounts are connected to the Internet so that you can sync settings, documents and purchases across devices. You create connected accounts simply by adding a new or existing Microsoft account to your device.

Creating a Connected Account

1. CLICK Start, , then CLICK Family & Other Users.
2. Under Other Users, CLICK Add Someone Else To This PC.
3. TYPE the email address or phone number of the user to add, then CLICK Next.
4. If the user doesn't already have a Microsoft account, CLICK Sign Up For A New One, then follow the prompts. Otherwise, simply follow the prompts.

Creating a Local Account

If you want to create a local account that isn't Internet-connected:

1. CLICK Start, , then CLICK Family & Other Users.
2. Under Other Users, CLICK Add Someone Else To This PC.
3. CLICK The Person I Want To Add Doesn't Have An Email Address.
4. CLICK Add A User Without A Microsoft Account, then follow the prompts.

Changing Account Pictures

1. CLICK Start, , then CLICK Accounts. Your current picture (if any) is shown.
2. CLICK Browse to select a picture or CLICK Camera to create a new picture.
3. Follow the prompts.

Changing Your Password or PIN

1. CLICK Start, , then CLICK Accounts.
2. CLICK Sign-In Options.
3. Under Password, PIN or Picture, CLICK Change.
4. Follow the prompts.

Changing Account Types

Users can have either standard accounts or administrator accounts.

1. CLICK Start, , then CLICK Accounts.

2. Under Other Users, CLICK the account to change.
3. CLICK Change Account Type.
4. CLICK the Account Type list, then select account type.

Removing Accounts

1. CLICK Start, ⚙️, then CLICK Accounts.
2. Under Other Users, CLICK the account to remove.
3. CLICK Remove, then CLICK Delete Account And Data.

Recovering Your Microsoft Password

1. CLICK 🅴, then enter the web address as
   https://account.live.com/password/reset.
2. CLICK I Forgot My Password
3. CLICK Next and follow the prompts.

Recovering Your Local Account Password

1. Log out and sign-in with a different account.
2. TYPE User Accounts in the Search box, then PRESS Enter.
3. CLICK Manage Another Account.
4. CLICK your account you, then CLICK Reset Password.
5. Type, then confirm the new password.

Connecting to Wi-Fi

Most Windows devices have wireless adapters for establishing Wi-Fi connections.

Connecting to Public Wi-Fi

1. CLICK ![wifi icon], then CLICK the Wi-Fi connection to use.
2. CLICK Connect.

> **Tip**: If sign-in is required, your browser should open.
> Accept the terms and CLICK the sign-in button.

Connecting to Private Wi-Fi

1. CLICK ![wifi icon], then CLICK the Wi-Fi connection to use.
2. CLICK Connect. Note that the Connect Automatically option is selected by default.
3. Enter the network security key, then CLICK Next.

Entering and Exiting Airplane Mode

1. CLICK ![wifi icon], then CLICK the Wi-Fi connection to use.
2. CLICK Airplane mode to toggle the mode on or off.

Airplane mode doesn't disable Bluetooth. To protect your device, you also may want to disable Bluetooth:

1. CLICK ![up arrow icon], then CLICK Bluetooth Devices.
2. CLICK Open Settings, then clear the Allow Bluetooth Devices To Find... option.

Disconnecting from Wi-Fi

1. CLICK ![Wi-Fi icon], then CLICK the Wi-Fi connection.
2. CLICK Disconnect.

Forgetting a Wi-Fi Connection

Your device keeps a history of Wi-Fi connections your device has used. To remove this history and any associated network keys, access Manage Known Networks options.

1. CLICK ![Wi-Fi icon], then CLICK Network Settings.
2. CLICK Manage Wi-Fi Settings.
3. CLICK a connection, then CLICK Forget.

Commonly Used Windows Key Shortcuts

+ A opens the Action Center sidebar. See **Action Center and Notifications**.

+ D hides open apps to reveal the desktop or reveals the open apps that were hidden.

+ E opens File Explorer.

+ H opens the Share sidebar, allowing you to share a screenshot of the open app.

+ I opens Settings.

+ K opens the Connect sidebar for connecting Bluetooth, wireless or WiGig devices.

+ L signs you out of Windows. See **Exiting Windows**.

+ P opens Project sidebar for selecting display options for multiple monitors.

+ R opens the Run dialog box, which allows you to run commands.

+ S opens the Search box so you can perform a search. See **Searching for Apps, Settings and More**.

+ U opens Ease of Access Center, which you can use to make your device easier to use for those with disabilities.

+ X opens the tasks menu. See **Performing Common Tasks Quickly**.

Thank you...

Thank you for purchasing this book. If you enjoyed this book and learned something from it, I hope you'll take a moment to write a review. Your reviews will help to ensure I can keep writing. If you have comments for me, a wish list for additions or feedback about a topic you'd like me to write about next, contact me by sending an email to:

OrdinaryHuman.Books@gmail.com

With your support, this book will grow and grow, so be sure to look for updates periodically! To get updated content, simply delete the book off your reader and then download again at Amazon's website.

More Books...

Ordinary Human is hard at work on other books for Microsoft products. If you'd like to see a book for a particular product, let us know!

Notes...

Notes...

Notes...

Notes...

27241864R00039

Printed in Great Britain
by Amazon

Windows 10 for Beginners

The Premiere User Guide
for Work, Home & Play.

Cheat Sheets Edition:
Hacks, Tips, Shortcuts & Tricks.

Standard Ordinary Human

Solutions & Training, 20-year Microsoft Veteran